Leadership in Analytics:

A Customer Focused Perspective

Digital, Business, Marketing & Social – Enhancing Customer Care & Loyalty!

Achieving customer loyalty is a primary marketing goal, but building loyalty and reaping its rewards remain ongoing (Watson, Beck, Henderson & Palmatier, 2015) challenges. Theory suggests that loyalty comprises attitudes and purchase behaviors that benefit one seller over competitors. Yet researchers examining loyalty adopt widely varying conceptual and operational approaches. The authors examined the consequences of this heterogeneity by empirically mapping current conceptual approaches using an item-level coding of extant loyalty research, then testing how operational and study-specific characteristics moderate the strategy → loyalty → performance process through meta-analytic techniques. The results clarified dissimilarities in loyalty building strategies, how loyalty differentially affects performance and word of mouth, and the consequences of study-specific characteristics. Prescriptive advice based on 163 studies of customer loyalty addresses three seemingly simple but very critical questions: What is customer loyalty? How is it measured? and What actually matters when it comes to customer loyalty?

Buckley et al., (2014) research study argued that companies in various industries, including travel, hospitality, and retail, increasingly focus on improving customer relationships and customer loyalty. The authors proposed a new systems architecture that combines the textual content in social media messages with product information, such as the descriptions summarized in catalogs, in order to provide marketing campaign recommendations. Companies commonly build user profiles based on purchase histories and other customer-specific information; however, when dealing with social media, it is difficult to often match the social media users with the customers. In this regard, the authors addressed the problem of targeting individual social media messages for which no personalized profile information can be retrieved. The authors solution combines two disparate computational toolboxes for text analytics—natural language processing and machine learning—in order to select social media users for whom to target with topic-specific advertisements. Natural language processing is used to analyze the context of social media messages, and machine learning is used to analyze product information, with the goal being to match social media messages to products and ranking potential advertisements. To demonstrate the framework, the authors detailed a real-world application in the travel and tourism industry using Twitter® as the social media platform.

A few well-documented cases describe how the deployment of marketing analytics produces positive organizational outcomes. However, the deployment of marketing analytics varies widely across firms, and many C-level executives remain skeptical regarding the benefits that they could gain from their marketing analytics efforts. Germann, Lilien, & Rangaswamy (2013) research is based on upper echelons theory and the resource-based view of the firm to develop a conceptual framework that relates the organizational deployment of marketing analytics to firm performance and that also identifies the key antecedents of that deployment. The analysis of a survey of 212 senior executives of Fortune 1000 firms demonstrated that firms attain favorable and apparently sustainable performance outcomes through greater use of marketing analytics. The analysis also reveals important moderators: more intense industry competition and more rapidly changing customer preferences increase the positive impact of the deployment of marketing analytics on firm performance. The results are robust to the choice of performance measures, and, on average, a one-unit increase in the degree of deployment (moving a firm at the median or the 50th percentile of deployment to the 65th percentile) on a 1–7 scale is associated with an 8% increase in return on assets. The analysis also demonstrated that support from the top management team, a supportive analytics culture, appropriate data, information technology support, and analytics skills are all necessary for the effective deployment of marketing analytics.

A fresh research study (Xu, 2016) introduced the knowledge fusion taxonomy to understand the relationships among traditional marketing analytics (TMA), big data analytics (BDA), and new product success (NPS). With high volume and speed of information and knowledge from different stakeholders in the digital economy, the taxonomy aimed to help firms build strategy to combine knowledge from both marketing and big data domains. The study suggests that knowledge fusion to improve NPS is not automatic and requires strategic choices to obtain its benefits.

Järvinen & Karjaluoto (2015) study proposed that the benefits gained from marketing performance measurement are determined by how an organization exploits the metrics system under specific circumstances. For this purpose, the authors reviewed performance measurement literature and applied it to the use of Web analytics, which offers companies a metrics system to measure digital marketing performance. By performing an in-depth investigation of the use of Web analytics in industrial companies, the study showed that an organization's efforts to use marketing metrics systems and the resulting outcomes cannot be understood without considering the reasoning behind the chosen metrics, the processing of metrics data, and the organizational context surrounding the use of the system. Given the continuously growing importance of digital marketing in the industrial sector, this study illustrated how industrial companies characterized by complex selling processes can harness Web analytics to demonstrate how digital marketing activities benefit their businesses.

Erevelles, Fukawa & Swayne (2016) study argued that consumer analytics is at the epicenter of a Big Data revolution. Technology helps capture rich and plentiful data on consumer phenomena in real time. Thus, unprecedented volume, velocity, and variety of primary data, Big Data, are available from individual consumers. To better understand the impact of Big Data on various marketing activities, enabling firms to better exploit its benefits, a conceptual framework that builds on resource-based theory is proposed. Three resources—physical, human, and organizational capital—moderate the following: (1) the process of collecting and storing evidence of consumer activity as Big Data, (2) the process of extracting consumer insight from Big Data, and (3) the process of utilizing consumer insight to enhance dynamic/adaptive capabilities. Furthermore, unique resource requirements for firms to benefit from Big Data are discussed.

Wedel and Kannan (2016) research study provided a critical examination of marketing analytics methods, tracing their historical development, examining their applications to structured and unstructured data generated within or external to a firm, and reviewing their potential to support marketing decisions. The authors identified directions for new analytical research methods, addressing (a) analytics for optimizing marketing mix spending in a data-rich environment, (b) analytics for personalization, and (c) analytics in the context of customers' privacy and data security. The authors reviewed the implications for organizations that seek to implement big data analytics. Finally, turning to the future, the authors identified trends that will shape marketing analytics as a discipline and marketing analytics education.

To prepare students for the rapidly evolving field of digital marketing, which requires more and more technical skills every year, a social media practicum creates a learning environment in which students can apply marketing principles and become ready for collaborative work in social media marketing and analytics. Using student newspapers as examples, Atwong (2015) practicum adopted an action learning approach to enhance student knowledge and skills in social media. The author described the structure, process, and tools that support this practical experience in a marketing course. The extent to which the practicum helps in preparing students is assessed and reported.

Berger (2016) study argued his own educational and career paths on the way to being a 'Marketing Analytics Person'. It also notes several 'Core Lessons' that the author believed are useful to anyone who is aspiring toward an academic career in marketing analytics. Some of these pertain to educational choices, while others to choices during one's professorial career. The article spans a time period of more than a half-century.

Jobs, Aukers & Gilfoil (2015) study demonstrated how the emergence of big data is driving the adoption of broader and increasingly sophisticated quantitative analysis techniques across media channels by large, medium and even smaller sized firms. A new ecosystem of marketing and advertising service firms is emerging. This ecosystem provides information processing services which impact marketing organization spending patterns in much faster time intervals than ever seen in the history of modern marketing. The findings of this study are a direct result of semi-structured interviews of stakeholders in the advertising analytics and related industries during the summer of 2014.

Dow (2013) argued that mobile marketing and commerce is gaining prominence in Canada, but companies that do not understand the needs and preferences of their customers risk alienating them in this highly intimate medium. Analytics helps marketers increase their knowledge of the customer, enabling improved personalization of marketing to help build trust with the customer, which is important to the success of mobile marketing. It also assists in breaking through marketing barriers with location-based, hyper-personal marketing that is best able to reach the customer and be impactful. As the promise of the mobile wallet is becoming a reality, by owning the payment and shopping channels, businesses can garner extensive customer insight and turn around to sell them product the company knows they are likely to buy based on previous behavior.

Every time shoppers make a purchase at a store or browse a Web site, customer behavior is tracked, analyzed, and perhaps shared with other businesses. Target Corporation is a leader in analyzing vast amounts of data to identify buying patterns, improve customer satisfaction, predict future trends, select promotional strategies, and increase revenue. Corrigan,

Craciun, & Powell (2014) case study highlighted a situation in which a teen girl unexpectedly received a maternity-specific mailer from Target and discusses the positive and negative aspects of this retailer's data mining program. The case focuses on the types of data needed to identify changes in consumer behavior, privacy issues that arise with data mining, and how customer analytics supports marketing decisions.

References:

1. Atwong, C. T. (2015). A SOCIAL MEDIA PRACTICUM: AN ACTION-LEARNING APPROACH TO SOCIAL MEDIA MARKETING AND ANALYTICS. Marketing Education Review, 25(1), 27-31. doi:10.1080/10528008.2015.999578.
2. Berger, P. D. (2016). One man's path to marketing analytics. Journal Of Marketing Analytics, 4(1), 1-13. doi:10.1057/jma.2016.5
3. Buckley, S., Ettl, M., Jain, P., Luss, R., Petrik, M., Ravi, R. K., & Venkatramani, C. (2014). Social media and customer behavior analytics for personalized customer engagements. *IBM Journal Of Research & Development*, 58(5/6), 7:1-7:12. doi:10.1147/JRD.2014.2344515
4. Corrigan, H. B., Craciun, G., & Powell, A. M. (2014). How Does Target Know So Much About Its Customers? Utilizing Customer Analytics to Make Marketing Decisions. *Marketing Education Review*, 24(2), 159-166. doi:10.2753/MER1052-8008240206.
5. Dow, C. (2013). MOBILE MARKETING AND THE VALUE OF CUSTOMER ANALYTICS. International Journal Of Mobile Marketing,8(1), 117-120.
6. Erevelles, S., Fukawa, N., & Swayne, L. (2016). Big Data consumer analytics and the transformation of marketing. Journal Of Business Research, 69(2), 897-904. doi:10.1016/j.jbusres.2015.07.001.
7. Germann, F., Lilien, G. L., & Rangaswamy, A. (2013). Performance implications of deploying marketing analytics. *International Journal Of Research In Marketing*, 30(2), 114-128. doi:10.1016/j.ijresmar.2012.10.001.
8. Järvinen, J., & Karjaluoto, H. (2015). The use of Web analytics for digital marketing performance measurement. Industrial Marketing Management, 50117-127. doi:10.1016/j.indmarman.2015.04.009
9. Jobs, C. G., Aukers, S. M., & Gilfoil, D. M. (2015). THE IMPACT OF BIG DATA ON YOUR FIRMS MARKETING COMMUNICATIONS: A FRAMEWORK FOR UNDERSTANDING THE EMERGING MARKETING ANALYTICS INDUSTRY. Academy Of Marketing Studies Journal, 19(2), 81-92.

10. Watson, G., Beck, J., Henderson, C., & Palmatier, R. (2015). Building, measuring, and profiting from customer loyalty. *Journal Of The Academy Of Marketing Science, 43*(6), 790-825. doi:10.1007/s11747-015-0439-4.
11. Wedel, M., Kannan, P.K. (2016). Marketing Analytics for Data-Rich Environments. Journal of Marketing In-Press. doi: http://dx.doi.org/10.1509/jm.15.0413
12. Xu, Z., Frankwick, G. L., & Ramirez, E. (2016). Effects of big data analytics and traditional marketing analytics on new product success: A knowledge fusion perspective. *Journal Of Business Research, 69*(5), 1562-1566. doi:10.1016/j.jbusres.2015.10.017

[Updated - 2016]

'Social' Customer Relationship Management (SCRM):

How connecting 'social' analytics to business analytics enhances customer care and loyalty?

http://ijbssnet.com/journals/Vol_3_No_21_November_2012/10.pdf

Abstract

Social Customer Relationship Management (SCRM) is about people and relationships and demands a customer focus. This study investigates how Social Media (SM) has become an undeniable influence on customer care. Given the unprecedented reach of social media, firms are increasingly relying on it as a channel (Kumar et al., 2016) for marketing communication. The purpose of this study is to explore how engaging customers through social communities are having far-reaching effects on customer loyalty. Goldman (2011) highlighted that the powerful reach of SM is enabling loyalty marketers to extend their mastery of dialogue with customers achieving trialogue. Evans (2011) stated that marketers are exerting their efforts to understand Facebook, Twitter and blogging to get the rest of their firms aligned with their SM programs. Smilansky (2015) study found that 58 percent of top 50 brands post an average of 5.6 times a week on Instagram. The study was conducted using quality content analysis procedure of the web surveys, interviews, and case studies. This study examined three main questions: (1) how companies can leverage SM to strengthen customer care (2) how SM channels enhances customer loyalty (3) what are the managerial and profit implications of these findings for managers and researchers.

Keywords: Social Media, Social Customer Relationship Management, Customer Care, Customer Loyalty, Customer Satisfaction, Customer Choice, and Consumer Behavior.

1.0 Introduction

Early adopters are gaining real economic value from their investments in SM. Barry et al (2011) stated that customers who engage with companies over SM are more loyal and they spend up to 40 percent more with those companies than other customers. Ang (2011) highlighted that SM is now a game changer in the marketplace because millions of users have become enamored with this new medium. The growth of SM is phenomenal. The most popular SM is Facebook. In the space of 7 years, Facebook has grown to more than 800 million users (and climbing), with more users outside the United States (70 per cent) than inside. If Facebook were to be a country, it will be the third largest, after China and India. It is also predicted that the usage of SM for marketing in the United States will grow from $ 716 million in 2009 to $ 31 billion by 2014. However, despite the growth, managers are still uncertain as to how SM can be used in marketing, some dismissing it as more hype than reality. This is because managers are not sure how to monetize SM.

More specifically, this study examined the relationship between SM, customer care and customer loyalty. Marketers are working in challenging times. Never before have we been able to get so close to customers and engage with them in such a timely and relevant manner. Harnessed with

customer relationship management, SM can deliver financial benefits to companies no matter what sector. The benefits are
Centered on increasing 'customer insight and engagement' and are not peripheral but fundamental to driving business performance particularly customer care and loyalty. Financial benefits apply across the customer life cycle, in acquisition, retention, value development and managing cost to serve. In addition, social customer relationship management (SCRM) can deliver insight, which will help drive real customer centric innovation. Woodcock et al (2011) reported that the knowledge gained on customer behavior, attitudes and mood will help drive benefits throughout the value chain (Figure 1) impacting on suppliers (for example, forecasting demand) and intermediaries (for example, shaping in-store promotions).

Despite the growth in SM, managers are still unclear as to how it can be used to benefit their organizations particularly in the area of customer care and loyalty. Part of the problem stems from confusing customers with online community members through the popularization of the term 'social customer relationship management' (Social CRM). This term is a misnomer because online community members are not necessarily customers of the organization. A better term is community relationship management (CoRM) because it more accurately reflects (Figure 2) what people does in online communities – connect, converse, create and collaborate.

Getting closer to customers is a top priority for CEOs, according to the IBM 2010 CEO Study. Companies are vigorously building SM programs to do just this. However, are customers enthusiastic about firms brand loyalty using SM? Most customers do not engage with companies via SM simply to feel connected. To successfully exploit the potential of SM, companies need to design experiences that deliver tangible value in return for customers' time, attention, endorsement and loyalty. With the worldwide explosion of SM usage, companies are feeling extreme pressure to engage where their customers are paying attention to benefits. Baird and Parasnis (2011) reported that this hub of customer activity is increasingly virtual, located inside a SM or social networking site. Clearly, this is where customers are congregating and businesses want to be. SM holds enormous potential for companies to get closer to customers and, by doing so, facilitate increased revenue, cost reduction and efficiencies. As might be expected, our findings indicate SM initiatives are quickly springing up across organizations. Barry et al (2011) reported that more than 60 percent of Internet-connected individuals in the US now engage on SM platforms every day. The speed and access to information that they've come to appreciate has made them more demanding customers. For example, many now expect real-time customer service recovery and quick responses to their online feedback. Hyper-connected individuals regularly broadcast their opinions. And they rely on their friends and social networks for news, reviews and recommendations for products and businesses. SM leaders understand and appreciate the magnitude of the shift in customer empowerment and the opportunities and risks that these tools create. As a result, they approach their SM efforts differently.

Companies keenly aware of this global SM phenomenon, are feeling intense pressure to get in on the action. Nearly 70 percent of executives say their companies will be perceived as "out of touch" if they don't engage, and over half believe their competition is successfully reaching customers through SM. Not surprisingly, their rush to embrace social networking sites has mirrored consumers' adoption, with 79 percent claiming a profile or presence on a social networking site (Figure 3), and over half use media sharing and micro-blogging sites.

Many companies struggle to calculate an ROI on their investment in SM. Barry et al (2011) reported that without confidence in clear returns, have difficulty securing the funds needed to scale their efforts. Companies that most successfully make the business case for SM use a two-pronged approach: First, they set clear business objectives for using SM at each step across the customer corridor. They run small, contained pilots, carefully tracking returns to demonstrate whether further investment is warranted. For example, if the objective is to generate leads, the same metrics and measures used to assess the effectiveness of other marketing vehicles can be deployed to gauge the success of a SM pilot campaign. If the objective is to boost customer service, the effectiveness can be measured by service resolutions, relative cost and productivity, call avoidance and the ratios of detractors converted to promoters.

Second, companies further build the case by considering the broader value of SM. They articulate the value of engaging their customers where they are increasingly spending time and consider the real business value that authentic engagement can create. Again, customers who engage with companies over SM are more loyal and they spend 20 percent to 40 Percent more with those companies than other customers do. SM platforms are becoming increasingly important for companies to engage with, delight and retain their best customers.

However, using SM as a channel for customer engagement raises interesting challenges for traditional customer relationship management (CRM) approaches. Baird and Parasnis (2011) reported that CRM strategy, enabled by processes and technologies, is designed to manage customer relationships as a means for extracting the greatest value from customers over the lifetime of the relationship. These strategies typically concentrate on the operational responses required to manage the customer care. With SM, though, companies are no longer in control of the relationship. Instead, customers and their highly influential virtual networks are now driving the conversation, which can trump a company's marketing, sales, service and loyalty program with their unprecedented immediacy and reach. The aim of this study is to explore the connectivity, conversations, content creation, collaboration and engaging customer metrics based on web surveys, interviews, and case studies of how companies use SM to manage and convert SM users to customers.

2.0 Study Methodology

Brand reputation is often determined by a customer's last experience with a company or its products. If customers have an exceptional experience, they will likely share it with their friends, family, and colleagues. The same holds true for a poor customer experience. Myron (2012) reported that organizations must regularly create positive—even exceptional—customer experiences.

Following the goals of the study, this research is built on previous works of Hutton and Fosdick (2011); Ang (2011); Baird and Parasnis (2011); Valentini et al (2011); Woodcock et al (2011);

Barry et al, (2011); Moran and Gossieaux (2010); Barnes (2009) using the quality content analysis procedure of the web surveys, interviews and the case studies.

A survey of more than 3,000 consumers conducted by Barry et al (2011) of Bain and Company helped to identify what makes SM effective. This survey found that customers who engage with companies over SM spend 20 percent to 40 percent more money with those companies than other customers (Figure 4). They also demonstrate a deeper emotional commitment to the companies, granting them an average 33 point's higher Net Promoter Score (NPS), a common measure of customer loyalty.

In October 2010, Baird and Parasnis (2011) conducted two online surveys:
The first was completed by 1,056 consumers in the United States, Canada, the United Kingdom, France, Germany, India, China, Australia and Brazil. Participants represented a distribution of ages among Generation Y, Generation X and Baby Boomers, with annual household incomes from US$25,000 to more than US$100,000.

The second survey went to 351 business executives in the same countries (except Canada). Executives represented companies from the following sectors: Distribution, Communications, Financial Services, Industrial and Public Sector/Healthcare. In addition, to capture qualitative data from executives responsible for SM programs, 17 interviews were conducted in the United States and the United Kingdom. In partnership with Oxford Economics, a Social CRM blog was established to solicit feedback on Social CRM topics from SM and CRM specialists and other interested individuals.

Woodcock et al (2011) reported that in an interview with Advertising Age in April 2010, P & G Chairman-CEO Bob McDonald said that what made P & G successful in the past will not make them successful in the future. He wants to avoid the trap of leaning too heavily on the company's marketing legacy and 'it is one thing that keeps him up at night '. Increased focus on digital marketing, he said, is one of the keys to P & G's strategy to remain a leading marketer. 'Any medium that helps us create a one on one relationship with any consumers is what we want to do an end point of marketing (or at least on the journey) is a 121 relationship with any consumer.

Digital allows that relationship. I want a one on one relationship with 7bn people … where we can customize the offering '. David Hornik reported that P & G's explicit goal for 2010 is to assure that each of its brands has a meaningful presence on Facebook, as an advertising platform and a brand destination, and they are willing to pay dearly for that and while P & G's thought leaders expressed some skepticism about the efficacy of Facebook s 'engagement ads ', they certainly view Facebook as a must have for digital advertising and brand building. They did not quantify what they are paying for that exposure, but it is quite clear that the numbers are very big.

Moran and Gossieaux (2010) in conjunction with the Society for New Communications research conducted "The Tribalization of Business Study" ("Tribalization") in 2008 and 2009. The study is composed of a survey and telephone interviews. The tribalization examined three factors:

- How organizations are establishing (or sponsoring) online communities;
- How the sponsoring companies measure success;
- How these organizations use their interaction with the communities to improve marketing and other business processes.

The communities studied range in size from fewer than 100 members to more than 1 million members, and revenues of the sponsoring companies range from less than $1 million to more than $40 billion.

Woodcock et al (2011) reported that at the WFA / RVD Global Advertiser Conference in April 2010, Adidas described how they recruited 200,000 fans to Facebook from one short campaign. Their spokesman said this would generate an incremental £ 13.2 m in annual revenue. That equates to 65 GBP per consumer per year. Leveraging customer engagement and bringing the power of multiple brands together into umbrella marketing efforts will be an important benefit for brand groups. In an interview with Advertising Age, Global Brand-Building Officer Marc Pritchard said P & G appears to have had a better return on investment from its corporate branding effort around the Winter Olympics than from many individual brand efforts.

Barnes (2009) research respondents were asked how often they use SM to learn about the customer care offered when considering a purchase. More than 70 percent reported that they engage in the pre-purchase behavior (Figure 5) at least sometimes. Nineteen percent of respondents rarely use SM to learn about customer care and 9 percent never do.

Barnes (2009) research indicates that there is a growing group of highly desirable consumers: 25-55 year olds, college-educated, earning $100,000+, a very powerful group in terms of buying behavior. These most savvy and sought after consumers are using SM to research companies. They will not support companies with poor customer care reputations, and finally, they will talk about all of this openly with others via multiple online vehicles. This research should serve as a wake-up call to companies to---listen, respond and improve.

3.0 Case Studies
3.1 Cold Stone Creamery

Baird and Parasnis (2011) reported that the Cold Stone Creamery's eGift program on Facebook is an excellent example of social commerce that optimizes the unique community aspect of social networking by enabling followers to send tangible gifts to friends. Cold Stone Creamery, an ice cream franchiser with 1,500 locations in 16 countries, wanted to find a creative way to engage followers with a valued offering and, at the same time, drive a measurable impact on in-store sales. From Cold Stone's Facebook page, customers select one or more friends to send gifts to, choose the product they would like their friends to receive, add a personal message and proceed through the security-rich checkout process. Recipients get a Facebook message ore-mail with the eGift and its associated redemption code. Following the instructions provided, recipients can redeem their treat and customize its flavor in any US Cold Stone store location. The results are impressive. Cold Stone linked SM interaction with concrete consumer behavior patterns to increase profitability. They monetized their Facebook presence by facilitating a fun, easy way for followers to send small treats to friends – something they believed their customers would value. They were right – within weeks, eGift added thousands of dollars in incremental sales to franchisees.

3.2 American Express - Small Business Saturday

Baird and Parasnis (2011) reported that American Express has two groups it wants to please: member card holders and merchants. In anticipation of the busiest shopping weekend in the United States, American Express launched Small Business Saturday, a program targeted at consumers to get them to patronize local small businesses. This clever campaign tapped into consumers' desire for discounts and their concern for their communities' economic wellbeing. At the same time, it provided support to small business clients during the peak shopping season.

Users on Facebook were encouraged to support the campaign by clicking the Facebook "like"

button declaring, "I'm in!" and sharing their endorsement with all their Facebook friends. To
advance the viral spread of the campaign, for each "like," American Express donated a dollar to a popular charity, Girls Inc. This charity donation was a significant incentive. Without having to provide personal information to engage, anyone could "like" the campaign and spread the word. Even on-card holders could click, key to creating affinity among people who aren't customers – yet.

On the program's Facebook page, customers and businesses could interact with "Shout Outs," and card holders could sign up to receive a US$25 credit as a reward for using their American Express Card at small businesses. American Express raised US$1 million for charity, extended the $25credit offer to the end of the year and encouraged fans to participate in polls about their experience.

4.0 Analysis

Barry et al (2011) highlighted that as social networking services such as Facebook and Twitter broke loose on the mainstream business scene, the majority of companies stood on the sidelines trying to make sense of it all. Despite the proliferation of corporate Facebook pages and Twitter accounts during the last couple of years, most businesses still effectively remain on the sidelines. The gap between the early adopters and those waiting to take the plunge has actually widened. While the average billion-dollar company spends $750,000 a year on SM, according to Bain & Company analysis, some early adopters such as Dell, Wal-Mart, Starbucks, JetBlue and American Express invest significantly more. In some instances, the investment is tens of millions of dollars. Who is right—the early adopters or the companies still waiting it out?

Research conducted by Barry et al (2011) also shows that several early adopters have captured real economic value from their investments. But the SM scene is so turbulent and frothy that many others have poured good money after bad in their attempts to engage customers. The leaders typically employ the same tried-and-true business principles—refined through traditional marketing, service and operations—applied in new ways. While they often experiment and sometimes fail, they don't allow themselves to fall into the trap of thinking that somehow "everything has changed" in this new world. As part of a broader customer engagement strategy, SM can be an effective and cost-efficient marketing, sales, service, insight and retention tool.

SM shouldn't be viewed as a mere channel for marketing or public relations or as simply an effective customer service tool. While many companies started out using SM to get the word out about products, the most successful have significantly expanded their efforts to engage their customers at every step of what we call the "customer corridor," touch points that start when a potential customer first learns of a product and extend through the moment they opt to make repeat purchases.

Several companies have registered real bottom-line results from their SM efforts (Figure 6). Most impressive, however, are the companies such as Ford, eBay, and Nike that have stepped back and deployed holistic SM strategies aimed at unlocking value at each stage of the customer corridor.

Ang (2011) reported that the principal objective of the CRM is to manage customer relationships so as to maximize their life-time value for the organization. This means, applying the right
strategic, analytical and operational tools so that the management of customer relationships is easier and in some cases fully automated. This includes having a 360 ° view of all customers, managing the customer lifecycle, developing customer portfolios, migrating customers from one segment to another, managing the customer experience across segments, developing and
communicating offers to the right segment at the right time to particularly enhance customer loyalty.

Organizations are increasingly using online communities to interact with customers, but marketers identify a number of key obstacles standing in the way of community effectiveness. Moran and Gossieaux (2010) analysis of the results of the Tribalization of Business suggest that marketers should understand key human characteristics as thoroughly as the Web 2.0 and SM tools they employ when interacting with customers through
Online communities and that by keeping these human attributes in mind, marketers may foster more successful community deployments and customer loyalty.

Social networking, moreover, has become a global movement. Managing a social networking profile particularly when the focus is adjusted to concentrate on larger markets—specifically, the United States; Brazil, Russia, India, and China (the BRIC countries); and the European Union "Big 5"(France, Germany, Italy, Spain, and the United Kingdom) a distinctive pattern emerges. So, why people join brand communities? Nine motivational factors were identified by Hutton and Fosdick (2011) — among them "To support a cause I like" and "To feel part of a like-minded community." To determine regional drivers they cross-indexed those factors (Figure 7) with five broad-based global markets: Latin America; Middle East and Africa; Asia and Oceania; North America; and Europe.

When turning to the analytics used to measure community success, however, relatively blunt instruments—"number of 'active' users"; "how often people post/comment"; "number of visitors"; "number of registered users"; "time on site"; and "page views"—are among the top analytics (Figure 4). Moran and Gossieaux, (2010) reported that since the majority of community members typically do not post or comment, the managers could develop better analytics (Figure 8) for determining whether the goals are being achieved.

As an example of how micro-blogging drives media meshing, Twitter regularly offers near real-time global rankings of "tweets" on its service. During the 2011 Super Bowl, heavy tweeting—or micro-blogging—began soon after the first commercial break. The global Twitter Top 10 Tweet rankings (Figure 9) featured UGC in support of such advertised brands as Carmax and Stella Artois and for commercials that supported a number of feature films, including "Fast 5," "Cowboys & Aliens," and "Limitless".

Ang (2011) reported that organizations can take advantage of these predispositions by using marketing research and public relations, nurturing opinion leaders or advocates, placing and creating advertisements, developing new products, lowering the cost-to serve, building brand

loyalty and sales, and amplifying buzz and visibility for the organization. SM holds enormous potential for companies to get closer to customers and, by doing so, facilitate increased revenue, cost reduction and efficiencies. However, using SM as a channel for customer engagement raises interesting challenges for traditional CRM approaches. CRM strategy, enabled by processes and technologies, is designed to manage customer relationships as a means for extracting the greatest value from customers over the lifetime of the relationship. These strategies typically concentrate on the operational responses
required to manage the customer. With SM, though, companies are no longer in control of the relationship. Baird and Parasnis (2011) reported that customers and their highly influential virtual networks instead are now driving the conversation, which can trump a company's marketing, sales and service efforts with their unprecedented immediacy and reach.

Valentini et al (2011) reported that the growing number of sales channels through which customers can make purchases has made it imperative for managers to understand how customers decide which channels to use. However, this presents a significant challenge because there is reason to believe the channel decision process evolves over the lifetime of the customer.

Dell's current SM efforts grew out of the company's customer-centric and direct selling model, founder Michael Dell's foresight of the power of online social engagement, and some infamous prodding on technology blogs. Brought to life as a way to respond to customer service issues, Dell's SM efforts expanded in multiple directions, helping the company increase revenues and retain loyal customers. To boost sales, the company's Dell Outlet site offers flash promotions through Twitter. The computer maker uses feedback generated on SM to improve its products and customer service: Direct2Dell facilitates active dialogue between customers and company leaders, while its IdeaStorm.com enables crowd-sourced ideas and gives customers the opportunity to collaborate and prioritize product and service improvements.

Finally, the company relies on SM to activate promoters and acquire new customers:
@Dell interacts with potential customers—and also facilitates promoter interaction with potential customers. End-to-end, SM is a key tool in Dell's customer engagement strategy.
Winning companies have learned that, while an effective SM strategy can reap big rewards, it also isn't something that happens easily. It is obvious to many companies now that you can't just put up a Facebook page and start broadcasting content. You can't take for granted that fans will just stick around and allow their walls to be filled with marketing and promotions.

Research conducted by Barry et al (2011) identified ten segments of social consumers (Figure 10). Members of these segments frequent different SM platforms and prefer different types of content and engagement models.

Companies such as Disney, Wal-Mart and Mattel, who target "moms," will find they are disproportionately "Social Butterflies" and "Social Gamers." A key demographic on Facebook, "moms" as a group spend significant amounts of time playing social games. Companies such as Nestlé have found ways to embed their brands into the games that moms play online.

The company allows users to grow ingredients of its Stouffer's brand prepared meals within the FarmVille game. It engages with key customers in the right platform, and with the content those customers find compelling. Alternatively, companies looking to capture the online attention of the "Young and Mobile" will reach them through micro-blogs and location-based games, making the most of the platforms that are popular with his segment. As the SM ecosystem continues to evolve, it will likely further fragment, making consumer segmentation—and tailored SM approaches—even more important for success. In addition to tailoring efforts to key customers, companies need engagement plans that explicitly target their promoters and detractors, as well as key influencers. Promoters are a company's natural fans, though our research shows that a company's Facebook fans and Twitter followers are actually a mix of promoters, passives and detractors.

Many companies today have social efforts siloed across functions. Leaders align their organizations to more effectively coordinate and communicate. Companies must make it a priority to increase the number of their promoters and shrink the number of their detractors, discovering and investing behind the actions that improve the company's NPS in ways that are financially sound and that will result in profitable, sustainable, organic growth. Once a company has linked its approach to business strategy and targeted its key customers, it needs to put in place an organization to follow through—an organization that's designed to enable coordination and share best practices. Winning companies mobilize cross-functional teams spanning marketing, sales, public relations, corporate strategy, customer service, product development, IT, HR and legal.

5.0 Conclusions

5.1. Key Results

The rise of the SM has led to a fundamental shift in the way businesses of all sizes engage with their customers. Lea (2012) reported that the firms rather than focusing on "touch points" during the marketing and sales process are using social technologies to form meaningful, ongoing relationships that involve frequent online interactions, often times through social channels.

The central questions of this study are as follows (1) how companies can leverage SM to strengthen customer care (2) how SM channels enhances customer loyalty (3) what are the managerial and profit implications of these findings for managers and researchers.

The most important conceptual contribution of this work is that the customers who engage with companies over SM are more loyal and they spend more with those companies than other customers.

Generally, companies should think about measuring performance and tracking results in three key ways:

> • Engagement metrics. Companies find it valuable to track the percentage of customers "engaged"—looking at such basic measures as site traffic, fans and followers. Additional engagement metrics include buzz and share of voice. While most companies rely on third party analytics firms to capture these metrics, leaders such as Dell and Gatorade have invested in their own SM listening command centers. Within these centers, employees complement SM monitoring software with a dashboard of key metrics such as brand discussions, customer interactions

and media campaign performance. These dashboards emphasize the role of listening as an organizational priority, and better enable companies to spot important trends quickly.

• Customer metrics. SM leaders invest in the tools necessary to track shifts in loyalty and NPS. They also invest in the manual "cleaning" of listening and analytic tool output to capture shifts in sentiment. Social analytics providers are still developing their machine-based algorithms to better capture sentiment trends, which are difficult to obtain with natural language translation (see sidebar: "A caution on sentiment analytics"). These firms—along with the broader set of social engagement, Social management and social intelligence support tool providers—will continue to invest to improve their tools. A further consolidation in this space is expected as the market continues to evolve and mature.

• Financial impact. Leaders aggressively capture personal identifiers to link SM profiles and associated behavior to customer records databases. Contests and promotions that requires registration of email addresses and Twitter "handles" help bridge social identities. Once the connection is made, companies can more easily track leads, conversion and ROI on social campaigns. In addition to measuring the success of social media efforts, those companies that truly extract value from SM "close the loop." They take the torrents of consumer insights captured via social engagement and relay them back to the product and customer service teams. It is this closed loop that allows

Companies to strengthen the underlying business value proposition. Ultimately, that is how SM delivers long-term, sustainable value.

Baird and Parasnis (2011) reported that the role of the business in the age of SM as highlighted by the IBM Institute for Business Value Survey is to facilitate collaborative experiences and dialogue that customer's value. The survey also indicated that the consumers are far more interested in obtaining tangible value, suggesting businesses may be confusing their own desire for customer intimacy with consumers' motivations for engaging. Furthermore the survey also emphasized that consumers have strong opinions about their SM interactions and, despite their embrace of SM, their willingness to engage with companies should not be assumed or taken for granted as:

- Consumers all over the world, across all generations, are swarming to SM, but most interact only occasionally. Despite the astounding escalation of SM adoption, only a very small percentage of consumers engage regularly by responding to posts and authoring content.
- It's about friends and family – not brands. More than half of consumers don't even consider engaging with businesses via social sites. For them, SM and social networking is about personal connections with friends and family.
- What consumers really want? There are significant gaps between what businesses think consumers care about and what consumers say they want from their SM interactions with companies. In exchange for their time, endorsement and personal data, consumers expect something tangible.

•The advocacy paradox. Most businesses believe SM will increase advocacy, but only 38 percent of consumers agree, and more than 60 percent believe passion for a business or brand is a prerequisite for SM engagement. Companies need to find creative ways to tap the power of the trusted social community.

5.2. Implications

Valentini et al (2011) reported that an important managerial implication is that mature customers will be less amenable to marketing efforts aimed at getting them to try new SM channels. Companies should therefore focus on improving customer care and incorporate appropriate SM channel design to ensure mature customers continue to maintain loyalty with the service experience of the channel(s) they have chosen to use. Barnes (2009) reported that these most savvy and sought after consumers are using SM to research companies. They will not support companies with poor customer care reputations and loyalty programs, and will talk about all of this openly with others via multiple online vehicles.

This study has important ramifications for managers. It is interesting to note that despite the strong feelings about researching products and brands and customer care, many respondents reported sharing positive as well as negative customer care experiences online. Several respondents commented that they recognize excellence by posting their good customer care experiences online. When asked which types of companies that have done the best job in using SM to respond to customer care issues, Dell and Amazon were cited more often than any other company. Goldman (2011) reported that in terms of industry segments, technology retail and travel companies were reported as doing the best job while utilities, health care and insurance were least likely to receive positive endorsements. The knowledge gained on customer behavior, attitudes and mood will help drive benefits throughout the value chain, impacting on suppliers (for example, forecasting demand) and intermediaries (for example, shaping in-store promotions). However, pioneers in large companies must overcome three hurdles: (a) organizational readiness, (b) over-hype and over expectation and(c) project management failings.

Moran and Gossieaux (2010) reported that the tribalization research indicates that creating successful online communities need not be fraught with the uncertainty or likelihood of failure some executives ' may fear. By examining the responses of the more than 500 companies that have participated in Tribalization, marketers can begin to understand those steps companies can take to forge successful online communities, enjoy deeper understanding of the customer, and foster greater trust between the organization and the tribes that matter. The Tribalization of Business Study provides some guidance on what elements of successful communities may include, but marketers should also understand hyper-sociality
to effectively market to their tribes of today and tomorrow for greater customer loyalty.

5.3. Recommendations and Next Steps

This study suggests that there is a need to carefully consider how firms can create a SM experience that is unique to their brand, offers customer value and exploits the power of the social communities. Baird and Parasnis (2011) emphasized that companies should consider the following to lay the foundation for a successful SM program that will help them reinvent their customer relationships:

- Firms must recognize SM is a game changer. For many companies, SM will become the gateway, if not the primary, communications channel to connect with customers. As companies design their SM programs, they need to think of their customers holistically and consider their SM interactions in the context of other customer touch points with the company.
- Firms must be clear on the differences between SM and other channels. Social CRM is about enabling engagement with the customer for the mutual benefit of the customer and the business. The traditional model of managing the customer relationship needs to adapt to the reality that the customer is now in control.
- Firms must need to make sure that the customer experience becomes seamless – across SM and other channels. If the firms know of its customer in one channel, it needs to know him or her in other channels as well. This means the social solution should not be devised as an isolated standalone program, but needs to be thoughtfully integrated with other customer-facing initiatives for improved customer care.
- Firms need to start thinking like a customer. Instead of asking why company should engage in SM, firms need to ask why a customer would choose to interact with a firm in a social platform. Firms are to recast social interaction strategies to focus on giving customers the value they seek and the customer intimacy will come.
- Firms are encouraged to explore what customers value most. Dialogue and participation is what SM is all about. Devising creative ways to capture the customer insights and getting

customers invested in the outcome will help build the advocacy and brand affinity.

•Firm must develop social commerce campaigns that target a specific customer need with time-sensitive offers or discounts that motivate customers to act will enhance customer loyalty.

SM is one area in which everybody is earning in real time. Just as companies need to continuously experiment to determine what works for them and their customers, they also need to negotiate an increasingly crowded playing field, with newcomers always joining the game. The companies that succeed will be those that are flexible and adaptable. They'll be able to quickly try new approaches and just as quickly adjust— or abandon them. They'll listen to social consumers and relay their findings back to product and service teams to strengthen the company's underlying value proposition.

SM still is in the early days and the gap between SM leaders and other firms as reported by Barry et al (2011) is likely to continue to grow. Consumer behavior will continue to evolve. New applications and social platforms will proliferate and enable even greater personalization and real-time, location-based engagement. Today's SM winners won't necessarily be tomorrow's. But amid the continuous disruption of a rapidly evolving game, companies that link SM to business objectives, target and tailor their engagement to key customers, build a coordinated organization, track results and close the loop, and stay flexible will significantly increase their odds of capturing real value from SM.

Acknowledgements

The author would like to give special thanks to *Chris Barry, Rob Markey, Eric Almquist and Chris Brahm of Bain & Company.*
The author is also grateful to the following individuals:
- Lawrence Ang
- Carolyn H. Baird and Gautam Parasnis
- Nora G. Barnes
- Graeme Hutton and Maggie Fosdick
- Edward Moran and Gossieaux
- Sara Valentini, Elkisa Montaguti, & Scott A. Neslin
- Neil Woodcock, Andrew Green, and Michael Starkey

References

- Ang, L., (2011). *Community Relationship Management and SM*, Database Marketing and
Customer Strategy Management, Vol. 18, 1, 31-38.
- Baird, C. H., and Parasnis, G., (2011). *From Social Media to Social Customer Relationship Management*, Strategy & Leadership, Vol. 39 Iss: 5, pp.30 – 37.
- Barnes, N.G., (2009). *Exploring the Link between Customer Care and Brand Reputation in the Age of SM*, Society for New Communications Research, Journal of New Communications Research; Vol. 3, 1, 86-91.
- Barry, C., Markey, R., Almquist, E., Brahm, C., (2012). *Putting Social Media to work*. [Online] Available at: http://www.bain.com/publications/articles/putting-social-media-to-work.aspx [Accessed 15 August 2012].
- Evans, D., (2011). *Social Media, Social Business and Social CRM*. [Online] Available at: http://www.marketingpower.com/Calendar/Documents/F%2712%20Training%20Series/f2f_SocialMedia_Bus_CRM_Nov_NEW.pdf [Accessed 25 August 2012].
- Goldman, S., (2011). *Trialogue: The Intersection of SM and Loyalty*. [Online] Available at: http://www.marketingpower.com/ResourceLibrary/Documents/Content%20Partner%20Documents/COLLOQUY/2011/intersection_social_media_loyalty.pdf [Accessed 5 September 2012].
- Hutton, G., Fosdick, M., (2011). *The Globalization of SM, Consumer Relationships with Brand
Evolve in the Digital Age,* Journal of Advertising Research, Vol. 51, 4, 564-570.
- Kumar, A., Bezawada, R., Rishika, R., Janakiraman, R., & Kannan, P. K. **(2016).** From Social to Sale: The Effects of Firm-Generated Content in Social Media on Customer Behavior. *Journal Of Marketing, 80*(1), 7-25. doi:10.1509/jm.14.0249.
- Lea, W., 2012. *The New Rules of Customer Engagement*. [Online] Available at: http://www.inc.com/wendy-lea/new-rules-of-customer-engagement.html [Accessed 10 October 2012].
- Moran, E., and Gossieaux, F., (2010). *Marketing in a Hyper-Social World, The Tribalization of Business Study and Characteristics of*

Successful Online Communities, Journal of Advertising Research Vol. 50, 3, 232-239.
- Smilansky, O. **(2015).** Why Instagram, Tumblr, and Pinterest Matter to Brands. *CRM Magazine, 19*(8), 21-22.
- Sponder, M., (2012).*Social Media Analytics: Effective Tools for Building, Interpreting, and using Metrics.* McGraw-Hill, New York.
- Valentini, S., Montaguti, E., and Neslin, S., (2011). *Decision Process Evolution in Customer Channel Choice.* Journal of Marketing, Vol. 75, 6, 72-86.
- Woodcock, N., Green, A., Starkey, M., (2011). *Social CRM as a Business Strategy,* Database Marketing and Customer Strategy Management, Vol. 18, 1, 50-64.

Figure 1: The benefits of SCRM.
Source: The Customer Framework 2011 - Social CRM as a Business Strategy (Woodcock et al, 2011)

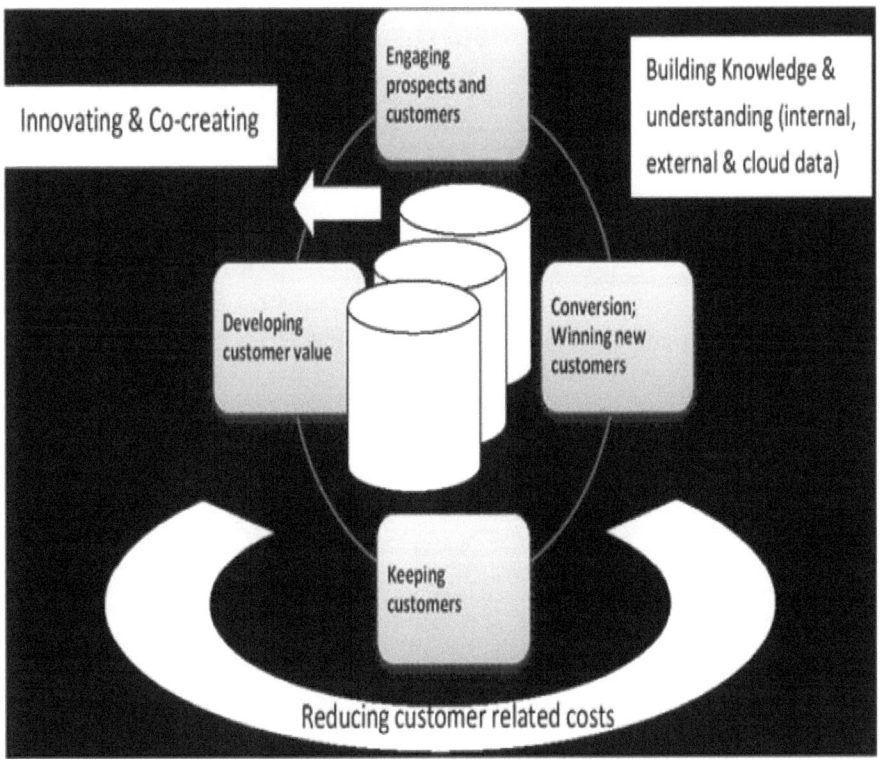

Figure 2: A schematic diagram showing the target difference between CRM and CoRM.
Source: Community Relationships Management and SM (Ang, 2011).

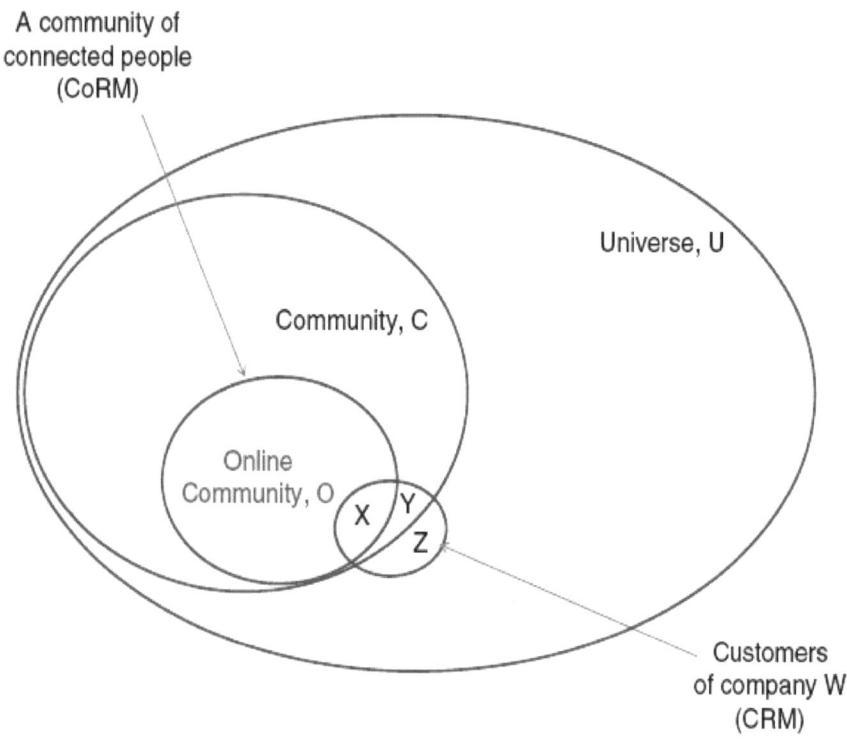

Figure 3: Companies tend to use social networking sites more than other type of social sites
Source: From SM to Social Customer Relationship Management (Baird and Parasnis, 2011)

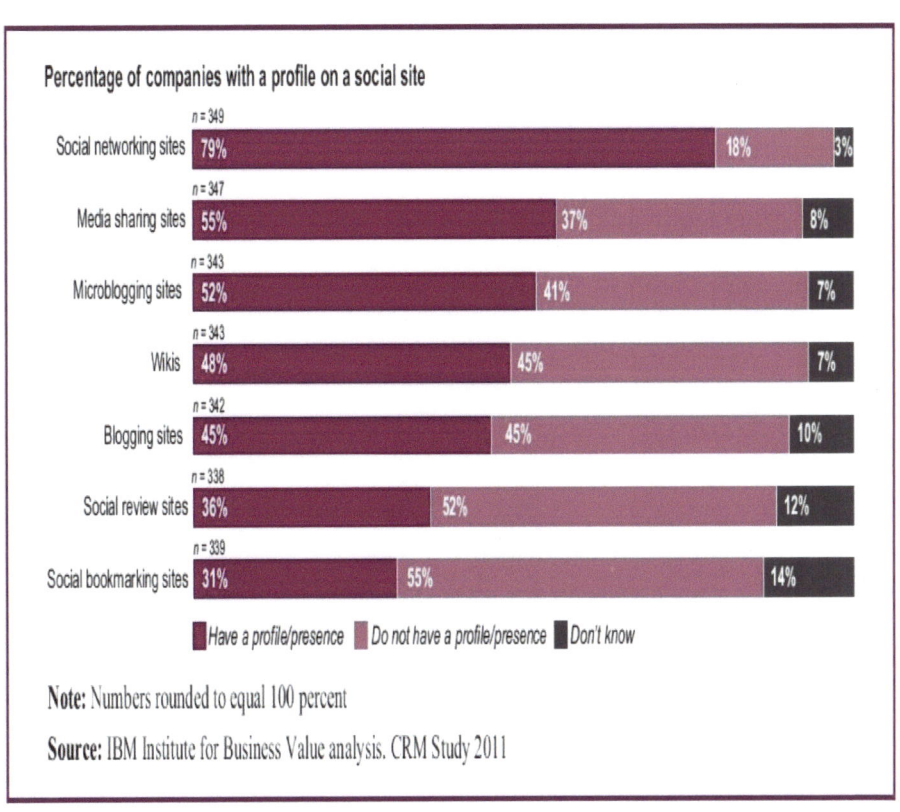

Figure 4: Engaged customers spend more - SM Consumer Survey

Source: Putting SM to Work (Barry et al, 2011)

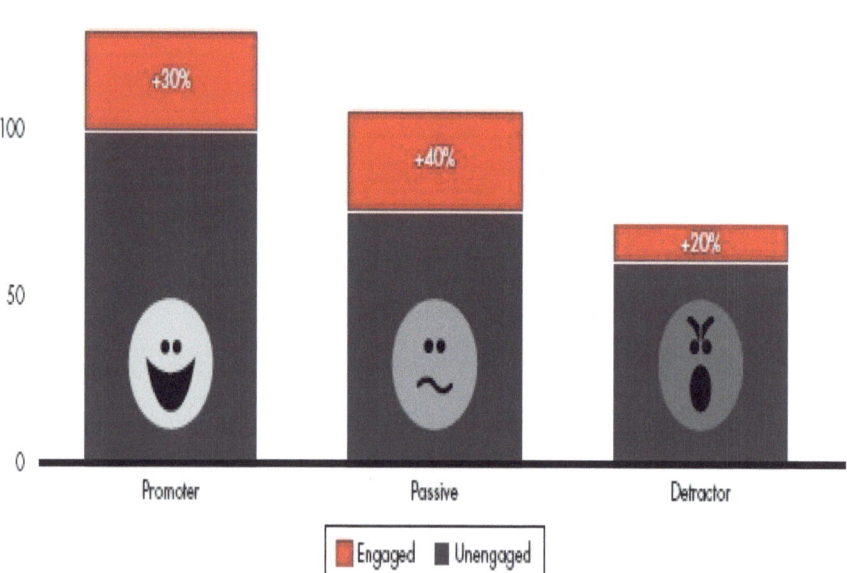

**Figure 5: Using SM to Learn About Customer Care
Source: Exploring the Link Between Customer Care and Brand
Reputation in the Age of SM (Barnes, 2009).**

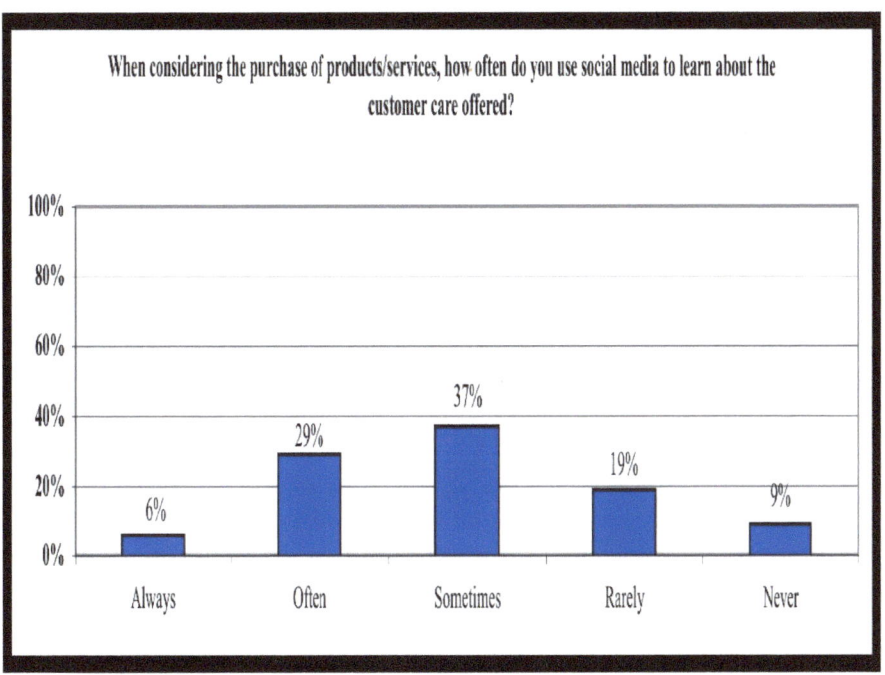

Figure 6: Companies using SM to serve the needs of customers can achieve real returns at every touch point.
Sources: Industry publications and websites; Bain analysis (Barry et al, 2011)

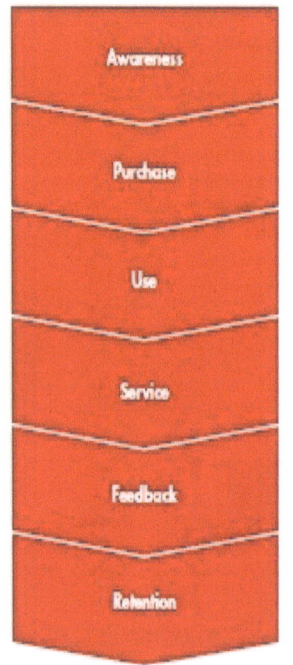

Ford achieved same level of brand recognition with a Fiesta social media campaign at 10% of traditional TV ad cost

Wet Seal reports that social shoppers have a 2.5 times greater conversion rate than the average customer

Nike+ product and social community credited with increasing Nike running shoe market share from 48% to 61%

Intuit's own QuickBook customers answer 70% of fellow customer service questions online

LEGO credits customer ideasourcing with its decision to launch more expensive and customer-innovated sets, such as the 500-piece Star Wars product

eBay community users spend 54% more than other customers

Figure 7: Consumer Reasons Cited for Joining Online Brand Communities
Source: The Globalization of SM (Hutton and Fosdick, 2011)

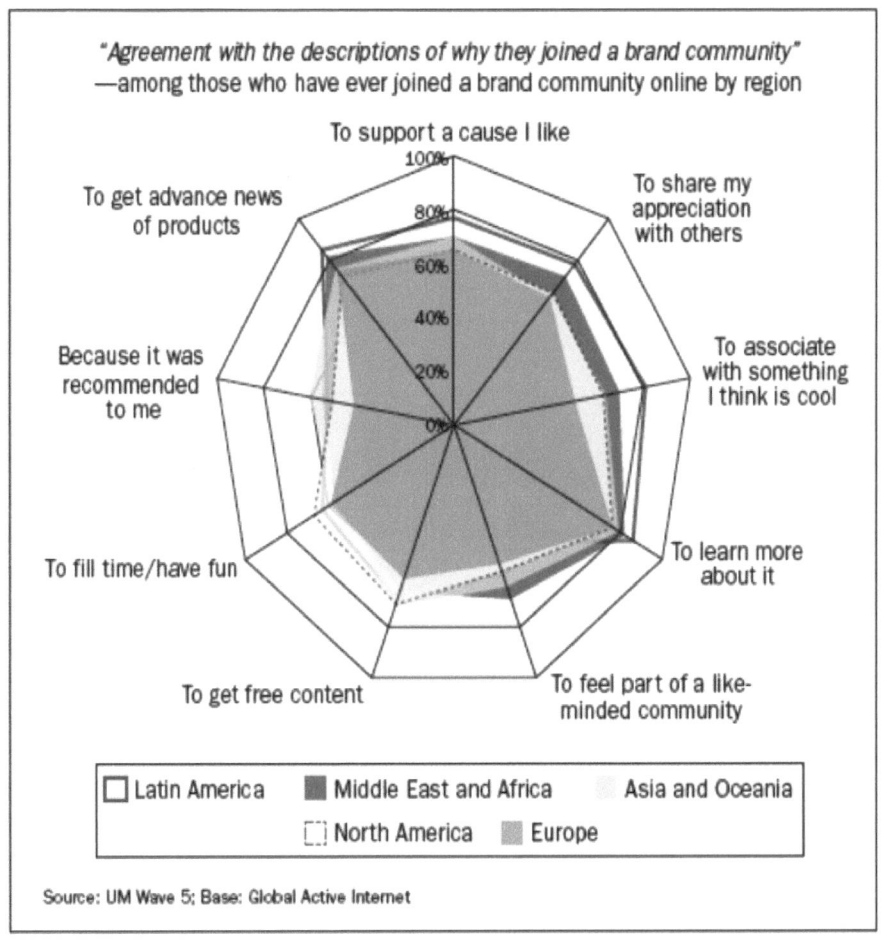

Figure 8: Analytics Used
Source: Marketing in a Hyper-Social Word (Moran and Gossieaux, 2010)

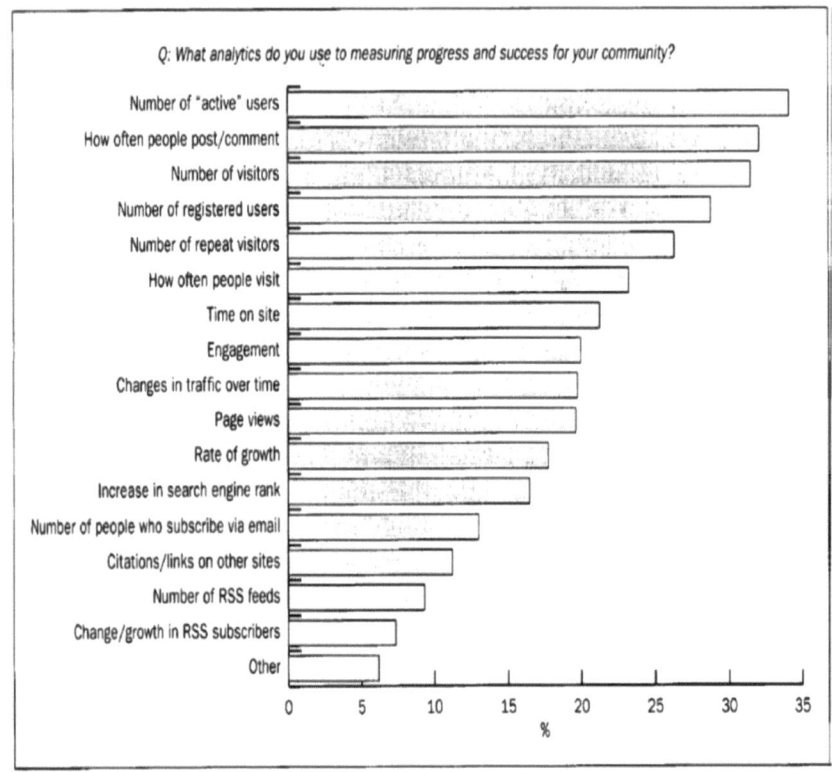

Figure 9: During the 2011 Super Bowl, Heavy Advertisement Tweeting Began Soon after the First Commercial Pod Source: The Globalization of SM (Hutton and Fosdick, 2011).

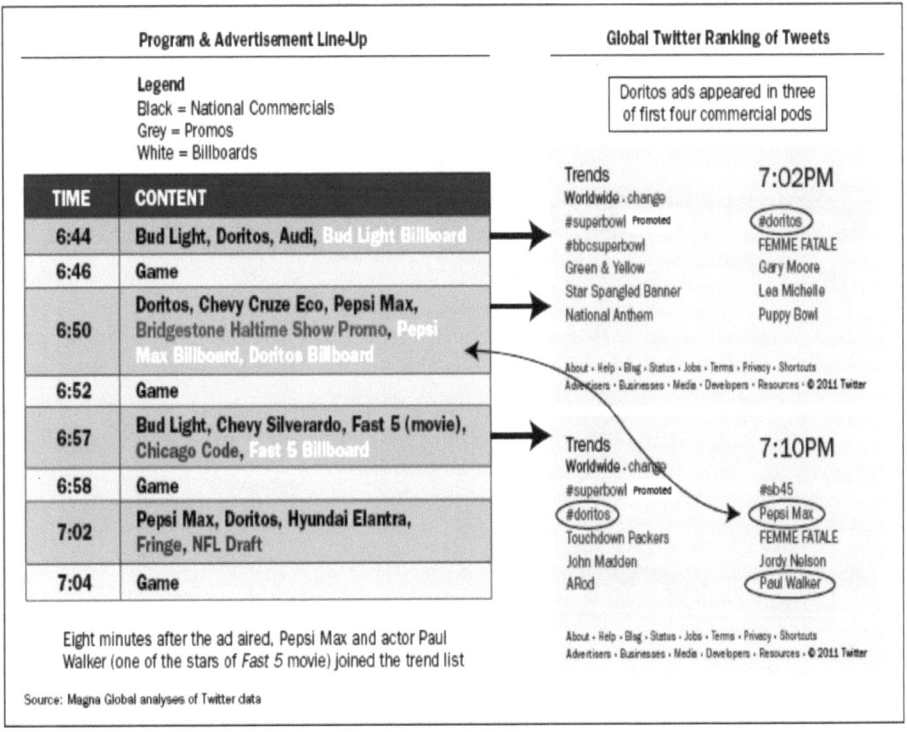

Figure 10: Who's online? Design the social strategy with target consumers in mind
Source: SM Consumer Survey (Barry et al, 2011)

Bain's social media consumer segmentation

18% Social Butterflies	12% Fact Finders	12% Contributors	11% Blog Readers	10% Observers
• Heavy users of personal networks • Skew to female users, younger and working • "Moms" represent a large share	• Heavy users of multimedia sites, ratings and review sites, branded communities • Skew to male users, older	• Disproportionate creators and posters of content • Heavy users of location-based games, crowdsourcing sites, branded communities, social shopping	• Moderate social media use and disproportionate presence on blog sites • Skew to male users, older	• Maintain passive presence on social networking sites • Skew to female users, older

10% Deal Hunters	9% Young and Mobile	8% Social Gamers	6% Showgoers	4% Professional Networkers
• Heavy users of ratings and review sites, group-buying sites, branded communities • Disproportionate share of spending occurs online	• Heavy users of microblogs, social networking and location-based games • Skew to younger demographics, e.g., students	• Active on social gaming and engaged in location-based gaming • Significant contingent skews older	• Tend to be passive consumers of entertainment and content generated by others	• Heavy users of professional networking sites and microblogs • Skew to male users, affluent

Google Scholar:
Social Customer Relationship Management (SCRM): How Connecting Social Analytics to Business Analytics Enhances Customer Care and Loyalty? Dr. M. Nadeem
International journal of business and social science 3 (21), 88-102
Cited by 23